BETWEEN THE TREES

© Kristiana Reed
All rights reserved.
Cover design by Kristiana Reed
Photographs by Kristiana Reed

No part of this book may be used, stored in a retrieval system, or transmitted in any form or in any means, or reproduced in any manner whatsoever without written permission from the author, except in the case of brief quotations used in reviews and critical articles.

ISBN: 978-1-7944226-1-2

KRISTIANA REED

For the girl who grew her hair past her shoulders

Between the Trees

AUTHOR'S NOTE **6**
FOREWORD BY SARAH PICKWELL **8**
I **9**

- *Grown Up* *10*
- *Between the Trees* *12*
- *Being Myself* *15*
- *What woke you?* *17*
- *Confessions* *19*
- *When I'm Dead* *22*
- *Red Tutu* *24*
- *Monster* *26*
- *Play Dead* *28*
- *Hurricane* *30*
- *A Candle of Maybe* *31*
- *Midnight Ribbon* *32*
- *Hanging Moon* *33*
- *Snow White* *36*
- *Therapy* *39*
- *Me and I* *41*
- *An Evening Bath* *43*
- *A Hot Chocolate* *45*
- *Mermaid* *48*
- *Sunset & Moon* *49*

II **52**

- *Ghost Boy* *54*
- *Cirrocumulus* *57*

Hunger 58
Today I fell out of love 60
Looking for I love you 62
A Wolf in Sheep's Clothing 63
Affection 66
I Knew My Mistakes 69
Bloom 71
The Vale 74
Last Night 78
She was a bird 79

III **83**

Aurora 86
9am 87
A Lullaby 88
Sherbet Lemon 90
Take My Heart 91
Vigil 92
Waxing Lyrical 95
Hands 96
Places for everything 100
Secrets 101
Luna's Love 102
A Good Thing 104
Aftermath 106
Reminisce 109
The Littlest Things 110
Breathe with me 111
You, me, the sea 112
At Night 114
Always 115

January *116*
Thousand-Year-Old Forest *118*

IV **121**

Aged Nine *122*
Learning to braid *123*
Whirligig *126*
Damsel *128*
Hope *130*
Perennial Blossoms *131*
Enough *132*
Sand Heart *133*
Inky Heaven *135*
The Allotment *136*
Kindness *140*
Home *142*
Spring *144*
The Meadow *146*
Beyond the Trees *150*

ACKNOWLEDGEMENTS **154**

ABOUT THE AUTHOR **156**

Author's note

A few years ago, I promised myself I would celebrate my twenty-fifth birthday creating and releasing a collection which reflected my life thus far. I think this book may be the only promise I have made to myself, which I have kept.

If the word catharsis did not sound so harsh perhaps I would have taken it for my title. Instead, the journey I have documented within these pages from depression to heartache, love to hope, is named after the first poem I wrote in years, age twenty.

Between the trees was written on a train from London to Essex, through silent tears, in a carriage bursting with commuters; most of whom were asleep or querying my upset, wearily. Moments before, I had stood on a train platform and prepared my heart for leaving; not the station but life, as I knew it. It took an almost goodbye to remind me how much I enjoyed the taste of living and smell of survival against all odds. Then, on the journey home, to my left I saw a field bathed in gold, lined by the edge of a forest. I saw freedom and I saw the cage I had built for myself.

For the first time, I saw a way out and it was beautiful.

And here we are, five years on.

I hope, dear reader, some of the pieces in this collection find a home in you. They have lived so long in me, it is time they moved on to someone new.

At least, at the end of it all, I now know how it feels to make and *keep* a promise to myself.

Foreword by Sarah Pickwell

Kristiana has been writing since she could first hold a crayon.

She would read out her stories with proud delight and as she grew older she loved her books and discussing the meaning behind poems. It was no great shock then, writing is something she passionately enjoys and has used this to express herself through both good and bad times.

It is hard to read your child's inner most thoughts at times; but she moulds her emotions beautifully in poetry and in prose. This book is my girl's story so far, and of the woman she has become. A woman I am proud to call my daughter.

I

"I fear I am not enough
to save the girl who always was."

Sunset & Moon

Grown Up

I'll be honest
when I said the words
grown up
aged thirteen
I didn't see
a tub of ice cream,
crying
and sitting in the dark
listening to the sky
opening.

I didn't think
I'd become
a rom-com movie,
the kind you see
on daytime TV -
hopeless romantic,
console me
with a cup of tea.

I didn't know
love and living
could hurt this much,
I'd prefer bees
butterflies
pretty flowers

and my hay fever
eyes to remind me
to breathe,
not this
tight chest,
I'm on my knees,
help me.

When I said
the words
grown up
I didn't realise
I meant to say
I've got wells for eyes
except I've cut all the rope
to the buckets.
I've got rootless flowers
for hands, so when the rain comes,
torrential or trickle,
I fail to keep it.
I've got a stained glass
mirror heart,
except every windowpane loses
its shine and bruises.

Between the Trees

My reflection in the train window settles
between the trees
beyond the glass
lining the field of gold.
The wind is whistling
and drowning
the thousand anxious angry voices
shouting between my eyes and ears,
between the trees
beyond the glass
lining the field of gold.
My toes are just within
the shade, on the edge,
gilded corn flexes its brittle fingers
coaxing me into the setting sun,
into yellow splendour,
away from this dim dense wood
in which I'm bound,
between the trees
beyond the glass
lining the field of gold;
touching life and yearning
for freedom.

BETWEEN THE TREES

KRISTIANA REED

Being Myself

It's been brought to my attention
I search for happiness in other people
instead of myself,
in a culture of self-love, self-care,
mindfulness and meditation
although they might just be the same thing.
I convince myself every morning
that I'm worth a reflection,
I to-do list my time
in an effort to ward off loneliness.
It's been brought to my attention
I have time to be myself
and not the companion of anyone else.
I know who she is, the taste of her name,
the way she smiles or talks through tears
in a valiant effort to feel normal again.
It's been brought to my attention
happiness is a choice,
a decision I can either make
or throw away,
but I'm picking through my options
like grains of sand.
I kiss them all with bitter salt,
let them scratch my knees,
fill the lines in my hands
and get lost in my wet hair;

dripping with perspiration
of waiting for something or someone
who isn't there.
It's been brought to my attention
I am on a journey to discover
the truth in being alone
I suppose I should start to look,

if only I knew where.

What woke you?

To the redhead in the window.
I didn't see your face,
as well as I would have liked.
But, my being on the street
and you in a second-floor window,
staring just didn't seem right.
But, it was 7am and the sun was rising
and there we were, two redheads alike,
already risen.
You, in all black, and I, wrapped up in wool.
The wind wasn't howling,
in fact, the air was still.
But, it was cold
and you had your windows closed
to the world.
I would have liked to have asked
'What woke you?'
Your hair was already pulled back,
severe and contained.
'What drew you to the window?'
with empty hands and curtains peeled.
Our eyes never met
and yet, in you I saw the woman I always see,
it was nothing to do with red solidarity,
but in the way your skin pales pastel
in the ever-reaching sun

and your bent chin spoke of the sorrow
which comes with letting too many people in.
So, I turn my head away,
to leave you to the peace
we had found together but apart,
two strangers with sunset hearts.

Confessions

I talk to myself,
no more, no less,
than anybody else
I'm sure.

I apply makeup
in the morning
for the people
in my imagination.
In regards to my first
confession, this probably
makes less sense.
What I mean is,
without it I'm invisible
to all things in
fantasy and reality;
so, I wear mascara
in case I bump
into a daydream
or a colleague.

When I'm nervous
I enjoy the taste
and texture
of my own skin.
I chew my nails

and their messy,
unmade beds
to the quick.
I grip my shoulders,
wrists and arms
to remind myself
I am real;
an open book
with a pulse,
intimidated by hands
with the intention
to close me.

I linger too long
in peoples' hallways,
on the stairs
and in the dark corners
of my memories,
and I travel through
happiness
like a bullet train
past rolling hills
and the setting sun.

I white lie
compulsively
to the people
I love, so as not

to hurt their feelings.
But, what does it say
about me, when
I am so willing
to hide all of me
from the ones
who committed long ago
to greeting me
as I am?

I write to myself
too. Poems, speeches
and stories.
Hardly any end up
on paper; neither
printed nor inked.
They exist and
they are gone.
Sweet bubble-gum
popped reminders
that I'm not okay
and I am okay,
often, at the same time.

When I'm Dead

These words will only mean
something when I'm dead.
When people are looking
for words about love
from a mouth
long decayed, buried
six feet underground
or scattered in ashes
into oceans and leafy gutters.
And my words
will become their words;
foreign lips breathing
life into lonely silhouettes
of love stories years old.

BETWEEN THE TREES

Red Tutu

I'm sat on a bench in a pub in London. I'm sure someone has vomited here, caressed the inner thigh of another here, spent the day drinking into five pm oblivion here. This is the first time I've been here and hopefully not the last. It's almost midnight and the pub is heaving. There is a band playing and blue, red, white and green lights play havoc on the human carved dance floor. A dance floor of questionable footwork which would usually be me. I would like it to be me. No matter how clumsily they sway, feet falling into gravity, they look feather light. Dilated pupils. Hand holding. The opposite to how I feel; smiling is difficult and so is walking. Talking is even harder and I'd like to curl up like roadkill. I'm not alone though. The seat beside me is occupied by the ghost who moved in with me this week - or never left, all those months ago, I'm not entirely sure. Each feathery fragment of my ghost is weaved from my insecurities and chooses to dress in violet blue. And sometimes, it lets me wear a red tutu. The red tutu is a chance to smile because you're happy, because you're you and the sky is blue or black and sometimes you can see the stars and sometimes the clouds will obscure the moon but you know it will peek out from the other side and make you smile. I like the red tutu but I fear I won't be wearing it tonight. I think the people around me hate me. For resigning myself to this bench with my ghost. I could be stood in the middle of the floor lit with colour and drunken laughter. I could accept the drink. I could say I'm fine instead of I'm depressed. I could count down the minutes in sadness rather than stay here to feel the bass drown out my heartbeat, and enjoy it. The ghost is holding the red tutu; passing it between its hands. It leaves me with an inkling of hope. Hope tomorrow is brighter. Hope I won't dream too vividly or if I'm lucky, not at all. Hope happiness comes from more than just sweet jars, home cooked meals and the way you look at me. Maybe, just maybe, it will come from the way I look at myself in the mirror, and smile because it's easy.

Monster

With those stars in your eyes
you see glamour in my dark heart,
you're blinded by the glitter of night,
the purple circles –
sleepless nights and selfish battles.

You call me purgatory,
sin wearing labels, bearing crosses
from your past life.
I am an escape to you,
something at which to gawk
and stare at behind glass;
watching how I flit in darkness,
a captivating menace.
But all I am, monster
of cliff-edges, bridges,
trains tracks, bathroom mirrors,
beds, forests and rivers,
is fear.
I am not a beautiful beast –
do not fall in love with me.

I am the sweat in your pores,
the lines around your eyes,
the creak on your stairs,
the damp in your walls,

the palpitations tingling
in every nerve ending.

I am blood.
I am skin.
I am a monster
because I am more human
than demon.

Play Dead

Monster is living inside of me
behind my ribcage,
she curls herself around my spine
draws her fingers to my throat
to stroke my collarbone,
to deliver raspy breath to my ear
repeating the words
on which I always choke -
my name, my wants, my needs,
my apologies, my fury -
and the dust from the bones
she's grinding with a gummy jaw.

Sometimes she sinks down
to bask in the darkness of my womb,
recline in my pelvis
and drag her nails up my thighs
and down my calves, towards my ankles,
where she binds me with manacles,
shrieking maniacally
words garbled with my sins -
breathing, praying, hoping,
talking, waiting -
for this torture to end,
for Monster living in my head
and the hollows of my heart,

to vanish and leave me
to play dead.

Hurricane

My woe spirals
like a wind chime
in a hurricane
and sings discordant
melodies only
a broken heart
could call lullabies.

A Candle of Maybe

I held my hair like a rosary
and pleaded with my nightmares
to be kind to me;
to burn a candle of maybe
whilst showing me every way
a loved one could pass;
to nurture hope
whilst teaching me the way
bones shatter and splinter;
to hold me close
whilst whispering poison lullabies
into the ears of my heart;
to remember I'm only human
whilst chasing me into the woods
where dark and dead things dwell;
to remember I'm only human
when I plead for help.

I held my hair like a rosary
and asked my nightmares
to be kind to me.

Midnight Ribbon

I tried to spend two nights away
from medicated sleep and vivid dreams;
fireballs and featureless faces.
I hoped in vain Nyx would visit me again,
tie me up in midnight ribbon
and suspend me gently
from her starry breast;
to listen to the wombing of her heart.

She came, cloaked in violet blue
and spoke with indigo lips.
Her words were harsh
like splinters when you're little
or cracks in every mirror you own,
and as I tossed and turned,
muttered words like these
and reached for the medicine
she reminded me she is the Moon's
mistress and the daughter of Chaos.

She came without ribbons
or arms to pull me to her;
she only brought darkness
and every thought it offers light
when there's no sunlight
to proffer hope of tomorrow's dawn.

Hanging Moon

Sometimes I wonder
which would be better:
death or insomnia?

Because I cannot
withstand the in-between.
Cold nights tumbling
in and out of dreams.
Dreams of dying,
dreams of living,
dreams of running
toward a hanging moon;
taking the rope
from around its pale withering neck
and binding my wrists
to the ground.

I want to lie eyes open
or forever shut
to worms, nightmares
and the shadows
which linger;
fingerprint silhouettes
of people I used to know,
of people I used to love.

KRISTIANA REED

I'd like to look you
in the eyes and smile
all night,
or never again,
at all.

BETWEEN THE TREES

Snow White

Today is Sunday and I'm by the sea. I'm wearing a Batman t-shirt; which is ironic because I'm in no fit state to save a city, too wrapped up in being the vigilante of my own body and soul. It's pleasantly breezy and quiet and warm. The sky is cerulean blue. Or, at least I hope it is. I'm toying with the idea of taking off my sunglasses; to pierce my eyes with holiday sky but I don't want to be disappointed by an aquamarine. I wonder if lonely walks to clear my head wrapped in sunshine are what being a writer is all about. Or, if this is just what depression is. Are those two things mutually exclusive? My sandals are digging in and I wonder if I deserve it. The woman to my left, sat on a bank of grass, is crying. She's hiding it well; a coffee cup, sunglasses and stoic lips. She is wearing red and I imagine her in a red tutu which helps her hear the crickets and birds easier and the crunching of my flat feet beneath her. I imagine her in a red tutu so she focuses less on the sadness she must feel in her bones and more on the coffee drips threatening to stain her clothes. My ghost has allowed me time alone today; time to smile, time to be quiet, time to listen to the sea and nothing else. I have brought the red tutu with me, stuffed

in my bag but now clasped in my hand. A father on his bicycle gives me the chance to wear it, to feel
its feathery tulle. He is cycling past with his son. Yards away he reminded him how to ring his bell, a warning, so I waited. I didn't look back but waited for the sound - small hands on metal and moved to the side. He thanked me and I smiled and with an absent mind stepped into the red band which matches my cheeks. The bee about my ear is much louder now but it means I'm not alone. In fact, I feel a little less like Batman and more like Snow White now.

KRISTIANA REED

Therapy

On our first date
I told you I'd dated
two before you.

The first, Liza
was blonde, stern
but held stories
in her eyes, yours, mine
and every fortnight
we sat before her fireplace.
I often cried and she held me
at arm's length,
preferring emails
to the confines of a room;
room I took up with my mess.
My unopened boxes,
my sellotape bandaged boxes,
my squished boxes.
With time we grew distant,
the tears stopped
and she had conversations
with my inbox.

The second, Mary,
we never met.
She knew I had a lonely heart

so, we talked;
about grief and change
whilst I watched birds
flutter and settle in trees
across the street,
her dulcet tones
soothing my sorrow.
We talked about blessings
and curses, what it means
to grow.
We never met, but I loved her;
for the time she spent,
an hour in my car
talking me down
and keeping me sane,
safe enough to drive again,
to make it home.
I suppose I'll always regret
letting her go.

You didn't seem to mind
you weren't my first,
in fact, I'm sure in your smile
and my sweaty palms,
we both already knew
you wouldn't be my last.

Me and I

My favourite place to write is in the bath. I have a cut of wood which rests on the sides, allowing me to scrawl like nobody's business until the pages are damp. Damp pages remind me of how squishy my feelings are - squeezing my heart and soul for coherent thought, art - and how porous paper is. I always listen to piano music so I selfishly wallow in tepid water and breathe along to my own words and only my own. It is always between 8 and 10pm: it's either midnight dark or sunset and during both, like a phantom, my mind soars to be with the birds in the trees. Birds, piano keys and bubble bath foam popping like candy are my favourite sounds. In between lines I like to scan my freckles for patterns, listen to the hum of traffic on the main road behind me and wiggle my toes at the surface. It's peaceful, me and I, I and me. It's the only time and place I remove the bandage over my third eye and try to see.

KRISTIANA REED

An Evening Bath

She's been sinking for days,
the ground a swallowing mud
she's lost all of her shoes in.
On Monday she was waist deep in regret,
now it's Sunday and the shame
is creeping up around her throat,
flecks of distance, good enough
and you should have known better.
In her need to be clean she draws a bath
perched on the toilet seat waiting,
nothing but time -
counting cracks in the ceiling,
tired of the solitary company she keeps.

Her filthy feet, cut and dried blood,
enter the water first,
followed by a tense waist,
ribcage cracked with sobs
and finally, her face.
Bath water gathers at her edges,
bubbles shrink pricked with oxygen
she struggles to exhale.
The tiles ask her for all the names
she was called today,
the taps drip condolences
in the gaps between her toes

and the porcelain sides swaddle her
as her mother's womb once did.
A smile slowly ripples across her face
as she is scalded;
her goosebump flesh prickling to red.

She could drown in steam and bubbles
for hours;
a hippo in a river,
a pig in mud,
a survivor and a giver
rubbing her scars
with dirty bubbles and salts.

By the time she makes her exit,
her skin is puckered and pinched,
and there may still be words
behind her ears,
decisions still clinging
to the roots of her hair.
But she feels cleaner,
braver, in spite
of the bruises and grazes
water cannot wash away.

A Hot Chocolate

I feel an emptiness but I also need to buy milk and tonight's dinner. I've made it to the shops but there is a coffee house here. So instead of milk and dinner, I'm hiding in the back, settled into a semi-circular swing back chair, with a hot chocolate and cake I can't really afford. I went for a small hot chocolate to prove it could have been worse.

I should have sat outside. I could have watched the world go by but today my world is full of judgement and heavy footsteps. Too heavy for my heart to handle.

This morning I felt on the brink of collapse. The worry I would go to work and my heart would stop, a too real and too frequent thought. My peripheral vision is yet to return and I think the female barista thought I was rude and the male barista may have been trying to get into my knickers. He said 'No, thank you' when I thanked him for doing his job. Now I wonder if he was thanking me because his toilet read is Customer Service 101 or if he liked the look of me or if he knew I needed reminding I exist.

I exist because my heart hasn't stopped yet. I haven't lost enough blood yet. It's as simple as that, isn't it? Existence isn't futile. It's the question on the exam paper you over think because it can't be that easy, surely? And so, those too easy questions become the hardest ones. The final hurdle we trip over into a track full of final hurdles. Life shouldn't be as easy as spending money you don't have on a delicious hot chocolate and hiding. But it is.

I know it is, because I just checked my pulse. My heart is still beating and ripples in my jumper tell me my lungs are still breathing. I'm existing. Maybe not at one hundred percent but anything above zero still counts.

BETWEEN THE TREES

Mermaid

It is strange. Of all the places I wear the red tutu the most, it is in the bath or by the sea. My ghost prefers to be near water. Perhaps the translucency, baring the skin and bones of all who venture in, helps it feel less alone. Or it sways in the coastal breeze and beneath the extractor fan, anticipating the sweet relief of leaving this world. The red tutu shimmers best underwater. I imagine it has sequins or it is a mermaid tail; and for a fleeting moment I feel beautiful. A flight of fancy I suppose. Or the final form I endeavour to embody someday. Everything will be red; her hair, her cheeks, her scales and her bath water skin. She will have a pearly white grin and her hands will reach hungrily for the dappled sunlight at the surface. She will be an expert swimmer and will no longer tread water. She'll float. She'll dive; headfirst, into life.

Sunset & Moon

The sun is always setting
and the moon already risen
by the time I am here.
In the comfiest loft
I have ever seen.
Through the orange lit windows
I see fields and trees
bathed in gold, bathed in a beauty
I have travelled miles in my mind
to behold.
The cushions are squishy
and the couch is firm.
An equilibrium of comfortable
only this woman and her distance
and her closeness can create.
She holds my heart in one hand
and a notepad in the other.
Sometimes she alternates between
heart and coffee.
She allows me to breathe.
Catch the oxygen
the tears push from my lungs
and into the cold fireplace.
There is space here.
I can touch it
and I can exist in it.

KRISTIANA REED

I can shrink in it
and I can nurse hope
and fear within it.
I fear too much.
I fear this fear
will keep me
from being bold.
I fear her words
will weigh more than his
and mine and the love
we've shared
in such a short space of time.
I fear our discoveries
will tarnish old memories
so they taste like wine
on the lips of a child.
I fear golden light
and the stars at night
are not enough to save me.
I fear I must get lost
in order to be found
but I've never been good
at reading maps
or trusting others enough
to let them hold my hand.

I fear I am not enough
to save the girl who always was.

BETWEEN THE TREES

II

"She used to look for I love you
in flatlining horizons"

Looking for I love you

BETWEEN THE TREES

Ghost Boy

It has been years since we met,
decades since we last touched
each other's lives with a smile.

Time has been cruel,
convincing me you were never
there at all.
A figment of a twelve
year old imagination;
lonely amongst the bookshelves
and films,
fixated on wheat fields
and sunsets.

You were beautiful
blonde and boisterous.
You made me smile
and laugh with ease.

You were the first;

to help me feel real
and worth more than
sitting on a brick wall
swinging my legs,
waiting for the one

who would never show.

Thinking about it now
you were so good for me.
My white flag
and life jacket.

You always had a zest
for life I envied.
You loved your body
and the music it played;
singing in the rain
tone deaf and innocent.
You were everything
I needed then,

and you're the friend
I wish I knew the way to
again.

Time is cruel and I wonder
if you feel this way too
or if you are half
to believing
this dream of me and you,
this feeling I miss
like the stars in the day,
was ever real at all.

KRISTIANA REED

Cirrocumulus

Sunrise
is my favourite hour
and today
the cirrocumulus clouds
and aeroplanes trails
shine livid white
like scars on a face.
I count them with pride,
wondering which trail is yours,
hoping you looked down
and waved
as the speed of flight
and goodbye whisked you away
to a home without names.
In all honesty,
it is unlikely
any of the sky dust
belongs to you,
I like to imagine
you took another route;
to avoid having to imagine
seeing my face
for one last time.

Hunger

You broke my heart
when syllables stopped
spilling from your lips
curled and plump
sounds which caressed
tightened
tendrils romantic
around my arms
ankles and throat
squeezing
constricted airways
my chest throbbing
furiously in the heat
hunger
between our fingers
and thumbs.

You broke my heart
when promise of a touch
became nothing
mutters
on the wind
sparks in a vacuum
fire
on the ocean floor
distance ripped

love asunder
insatiable hunger
sated
by another.

Today I fell out of love

Today I fell out of love
with butterflies and brunette eyes
with your ties and under the carpet lies.
Today I fell out of love
with watching time go by
with seemingly waiting to die.
Today I fell out of love
with always being stationary
with wishing on a dandelion fairy.
Today I fell out of love
with my past, present and future
and every ounce being held with a suture.
Today I fell out of love
with you, with me
with us.

BETWEEN THE TREES

Looking for I love you

She used to write I love you
on notepaper to burn it in the fire,
like wishing on a star,
she'd surely ignite someone's desire.

She used to witness I love you
slip out in secret at night,
leaving her alone
to turn out the light.

She used to look for I love you
in flatlining horizons,
scaling the highest heights
for the best view of silence.

She used to call out for I love you
in empty rooms,
searching for the deity
named You.

She used to imagine I love you
dressed in black,
in an open casket,
lying on its back.

A Wolf in Sheep's Clothing

It wasn't until after you'd left
me with voices in my head,
that I found your sweater;
mutton-coloured, merino wool
folded neater than I could ever be.

It smelt of you;
the neck was cut
and dressed
with enamelled beads.
In the seams
I saw your sneer
crooked and harsh.

I wore it anyway.
In solidarity with the love
I once messily kindled,
with the friendship I once tended;
as you softly brandished secateurs,
pruning to perfection
your unruly rose.

Even though it itched,
picked, at my imperfections
with a snarling grin,
I wore it for a day.

KRISTIANA REED

Like you, I sneered;
white claws drawing blood
from my lips.
Like you, I wore expectations
taught by an unfaithful father
and coddling mother.
Like you, I stared hard
at soles with the nerve
to walk upon this earth,
alongside my perfect feet,
dressed in you.

One day was enough.
To finally meet the wolf;
who had charmed his way
into my nightdress,
who had almost devoured me,
who had almost married me.
In clothing which made me messy
and he pretty – petty.

I pulled off your sweater
from the bottom;
unravelled its edges
like I broke your heart.
I burnt the remaining thread.

BETWEEN THE TREES

I burnt it, in the flames
of the ardour,
I never felt for you.

Affection

fifteen, naïve
and couldn't have known better,
still wouldn't almost ten years later;
she believed this meant
she had to pump her blood
like breastmilk,
bottle it up and share it.
you didn't want her
last sweet,
you wanted her first tooth
and the nectar
she kept from you.
she believed
affection was currency,
kisses to buy company,
hands to hold
a future in,
favours to build
a house with.
affection
made her swallow
her words and die
quietly with them;
a tombstone
for every time
she wished she had

said something.
she let you
court other women
and still call
her the one,
under your thumb.
she pumped her blood,
stored her nectar in jars
and allowed your lessons
to teach her
she wasn't enough
to be loved.

KRISTIANA REED

I Knew My Mistakes

I knew my mistakes when they were
emblazoned
across my chest, a red poker hot dress
you bought for me when I forgot your tea
or to arrange the flowers perfectly.

I knew my mistakes when both hello
and goodbye were pursed lips,
a cold shoulder in the sheets,
a clarion call of silence.

I knew my mistakes when you shared them
with our friends, your mother and mine,
a verbatim list of why you didn't have the time
to raise me an angel following in your wake.

I knew my mistakes when pity
felt more like love than kissing you
goodnight, lying in wait for you to finish
me - breakfast, lunch and dinner.

I forgot my mistakes when I said I was leaving
and opened the door for you,
letting the *useless* escape from my bones
to join you with your suitcase down the road.

KRISTIANA REED

Bloom

Only dead flowers remain the same,
pressed, kept in a frame.
And I am a flower in bloom.

KRISTIANA REED

BETWEEN THE TREES

The Vale

We talked more here
than at home.
It was the only place
I could look at you
and love you timelessly.

The silence,
was comfortable too.
No longer punctuated
with betrayal
and bickering about anything,
from the biscuit tin
to communism.

I guess
it's all worthless now.
It won't lessen
the distance
or depression.

I guess
I was naïve
to believe I could
come here to forget you.
Instead, I have brought
every part of you;

your eyes
and their cornflower sadness,
your crooked smile.

I sigh,
an exhale
breathing a bumblebee
into blue sky.
No one ever warns you
breaking another's heart,
tears yours asunder too.

I've felt ashamed
of this pain
because it was I
who left you,
and I've been losing
who I was with you
and calling it
by every other name
except 'healing'
from the wounds
of my own making.

I wish,
on a dandelion fairy,
this will all be over soon.
I scatter every memory

like ash
to float with the algae
on the river behind me.

And to a field
of strangers and quiet,
shattered pieces
and eternal sunshine
I say thank you.

Thank you,
for knowing me
and loving me,
for losing me
and forgetting me.

BETWEEN THE TREES

Last Night

Last night
I heard a voice
which I can no longer place -
not in memories nor in second chances.
I'm hoping this means,
I've finally forgotten your face.

She was a bird

In a few years' time
I hope we'll see each other again.
We'll be in different clothes
with difference faces and partners
who aren't you or I.
I will smile because
I've always been gracious
and I've been waiting for this.
You'll smile too
but it will be weaker, pained,
stretched like papier-mâché.
And I hope when your new wife asks
what happened between us,
you'll say:

'She was a bird
and I was a cage
of black bars rattling
with rage,
never unlocked
yet with the power to pluck
each feather from her wings.
She had always deserved to fly,
you could see it in her eyes;
small, beady and watchful
but if she ever stepped too close

to the edge
I would give her a mouthful,
of steel, rust and dust.
I wasn't good enough
so I forced her to believe
it was her;
her fire, her salt,
her brimstone, her faults
and her wings.
Those wings which refused to cease
and continued to beat
against the bars of my chest,
the crook of my arm
the back of my head.
She left me,
not because she outgrew me
but because she never belonged
in a cage in the first place.'

You won't say anything more
because on cue
my shoulder blades will part
for my wings to unfurl.
They are fuller, they glimmer
more than when you saw them last.
They are iridescent;
bewitching in moonlight,
spellbinding in sunshine

BETWEEN THE TREES

and they are mine, all mine;
the bird who was finally freed
to fly.

KRISTIANA REED

III

"and every love poem I write
is definitely about you."

Waxing Lyrical

KRISTIANA REED

BETWEEN THE TREES

Aurora

The sun rises in all places,
even here, across these headstones,
casting beams of sunlight
onto pavement and grass.
Everything is asleep,
except her, a lone wanderer
who likes the taste of seven am
and the way the sky blushes
as the moon whispers goodbye
and the sun, hello.
Everything is silent,
apart from her heart
which thunders in memory
of him.
The clouds are gilded in gold,
fingertip lining, a reminder
of the life she felt with him.
Much like these buried lovers
and their beloveds
above and below.
Shadow lingers, seeking
a home in the girl
lost in Aurora's graveyard,
amongst flowers and shades
of solemn remembrance.

9am

Golden sunlight shivered
in the pale rose sky
then shattered with gusts of wind,
squishy cheeked blows
scattering light and silver trim
left dangling from forlorn clouds
into a whirlpool of blue
blushing pink.
Frost stretched lazily past
my toes, sinking into dew jewels
and blades of Winter's heartache.
The seat, shrouded in shadow trees
reached out for lovers
to call its own,
and it was there,
we found our home.

A Lullaby

We curled into each other's lives
as if wisps of bottle blue smoke
writhing into the sky, tendrils
slipping to join hands, hearts and minds
a discordant lullaby made beautiful
intertwining music notes and audible sighs,
fingertips and toes and the ridges of our bones
tucked like puzzle pieces
into our unknowns – a lesson
in discovery and mansions
fit for lords and ladies,
a grand piano with shivering keys.

BETWEEN THE TREES

Sherbet Lemon

I love the way you speak,
the way your voice melts
like sherbet lemon drops
and your words weave tapestries
along my spine
tingling chills,
I adore your desire to pause
to breathe me
in
bearing enamelled claws.

Take My Heart

Take my heart
and teach me how
to sing a sunset -
to warble peaches and roses
as Helios sinks
and Selene rises,
from the loins of horizon.

Vigil

The book had been upon your lips for weeks.
It was shrouded in your love,
your admiration, still unclear to me.
In lonely bookshop wanders I thought of you.
Of the book, its title
and the way your mouth navigated
the sounds, soft and hard.
It lingered in the corners of our conversations,
presented itself into memories
I was forming with you,
like a petroleum sheen bubble
in a cloudless sky.

When you placed the book in my hands
it was the first thought you had.
It was like handing me all the knowledge of your world,
your first born,
memories of your first day at school,
how you feel when you walk along
a beach or a moor.
It was like handing me the darkest secret,
wiping blood on my hands,
a cake you had baked,
the essence of you.
It was like asking me to hold you,

BETWEEN THE TREES

all that you were, all that you are
and hoping I'd keep you.
When you placed the book in my hands
you granted my heart permission
to grasp the figment of you
I never thought tangible.

In my vigil of reading
you became every character
and the author.
Within these pages a past, present and future
dwelt.
The lines on your face traced onto yellowing
paper,
the printed ink a tattoo of thought,
of what I was to you or you to me.
In the beauty I found purpose
in the fated connection we didn't believe in
but revelled in, nonetheless.

My vigil was shared, this wasn't a journey
to be alone.
Talking to you filled the pauses
and line breaks. You punctuated
the beginnings and ends of chapters.
And in this transaction of words,
stories and people
you held me before a mirror,

a reflection of me.

The girl you gave the book to,
the girl clumsy and loving
who easily bends spines and sleeves,
the girl who sees beauty
in sunlit dust motes, in your hands,
the girl who smiles far too much
and never enough.

The girl who realised, with your book
she possessed all of you
and had fallen in love with you,
as you with her.

Waxing Lyrical

The clock hands move past midnight
and the witching hour
for waxing lyrical begins.
We talk about how
the jigsaw edges of my heart
fit perfectly
in between your fingers,
how we do not believe
in ghosts or past lives
but acknowledge the need to be
ever present in each other's,
how our feelings are sensations,
seismic emotions wrapped
and gifted unto our bodies,
how your smile is smaller than mine
yet makes my whole world shine,
how roses are red,
our eyes are blue
and every love poem I write
is definitely about you.

Hands

I run my petal soft fingertips
along the contours of your hands;
counting each line, stroking each knuckle,
tracing the inside of your palm
and the indents around your nails.
This is the first time I've held hands
like yours - gentle like a stream,
hands which wash over my feet,
my hips, chest and face.
They do not threaten or intimidate.
They are not calloused with brick wall,
or the space behind my head.
They are not blistered by his use
of my flesh for pity, stripped
of my humility.
They are not clammy
with 'love me or feel sorry'.

They are hands which call me
a queen and I feel it.
They are hands which refuse
to knock the wind from my chest.
They are hands which tend to
the soil below my waist,
allow my stem to flourish
instead of stifle.

BETWEEN THE TREES

They are hands which pull
back the curtains to bathe me
in sunlight, and in my naked fragility
I find sunflower strength,
not the love he saw
in my weakness.
They are hands which do not question
their purpose to hold.

They are hands;
not fists, not weapons,
nor bee stings, nor paws.
And when they open up to me,
I'm happy to be yours.

KRISTIANA REED

BETWEEN THE TREES

Places for everything

Your hand on my waist,
shoes by the door, head resting
against your chest.

Secrets

I listened to your heartbeat;
it told me secrets
I promised to keep,
told me stories
of kings and queens,
of your wildest dreams.

Luna's Love

The moon blushed
each time she saw him.
She curled the corners
of her pale oval eyes
into a smile
and bid him welcome.

He visited her each night.

Come rain or silver,
he blew kisses for her
to catch and stow
in the dusty hearts
of stars.

These stars shone ever brighter in the sky.

He visited the lady of light
in the hope of reaching
his love;
snuggled up and delicate
hidden and touched
only by a dappled ray
of reflected night.

He hoped a single kiss

of Luna's love would be enough
for the stars
to deliver his wishes;
kisses unto his love's
shoulders and cheeks
and his promise to always be there
each night she falls asleep.

A Good Thing

The radio switches on. 5.20am. The room is well lit from the rising sun through pale curtains. In the mirror opposite the bed I see my figure; milky skin and nothing else. The sheets have fallen well below my hips, just touching the midpoint of my thighs, brushing my feet. My eyes are slowly blinking and I'm breathing oxygen deep into my lungs; feeling the rush of air open every window and door inside me, pulling back every curtain and blowing the dust from every shelf. I'm awake and I turn. I turn like I do every morning into the other side of the bed. The other side which is always still made, duvet tucked beneath pillow and cold to touch. This morning, I turn and I find you. I see you washed in a morning peach aura. I see your blue, blue eyes; so blue they reflect all the constellations you see in me, even when I do not. You are there and you are perfect because your chest rises and falls in time with mine, because your arm is already tucking itself beneath my head and shoulders, pulling me to you, because I can hear the drumming of your heart in your chest and it is the bass to my own. You are perfect because you are here and we are listening to radio two wondering if this is how it feels when time stops, when the earth isn't spinning on its axis and wondering if this will be the one good thing we can make last.

Aftermath

You wash me down
with a cup of tea;
after you said it was your turn
and how much you like
the taste of honey,
after you listened to me
like I was spoken word poetry,
after you aced every equation
and traced every line,
after you conjured
every algebraic vowel
from my glistening lips,
bee sting mouth.

BETWEEN THE TREES

KRISTIANA REED

Reminisce

I want to listen to bird song
and reminisce about love,
about your touch.

Hands which are presents to open,
unwrapping each knuckle, finger
and thumb. A tongue
which unfolds like Christmas ribbon
in my mouth, brushes my lips,
a kiss.

The Littlest Things

You didn't close the cupboard door
upon your departure
and I wonder why that is,
as my eyes prick with tears.
Is it so, in closing it, I feel you
where you last were,
the contours of the brass,
your spine curved around mine.
Is it so I'm reminded that our future
is ajar,
not fully open or closed
but a breath holding in between;
a tight chest maybe.
Is it so I convince myself
you're still here,
your shoes still there;
you are just elsewhere.
Is it so I smile because you
probably just forgot
but you love me so well;
I believe even the littlest things
you do,
are for me.

Breathe with me

Without her,
he forgets how to breathe;
he becomes a shore
which only says goodbye
sending waves away
with seafoam kisses,
his arms are crossed
and his chest tight,
water pooling by his toes
never reaching his knees.
A lonely shoreline
and distant horizon
washed orange and blue
until she takes his hands,
kisses each knuckle
and the honeyed skin
below his ear and tells him
to believe
and 'breathe with me.'

You, me, the sea

I do not live close enough to the sea
to hear seagulls,
the circling squawks echoing
through a red brick housing estate
which only knows the waves of oncoming
traffic,
which only knows sirens flashing red and blue.

Nevertheless, I am grateful for their song,
their nails on chalkboard melody
reminding me of the distant ocean
which surrounds me even when I'm alone
toes in carpet not sand,
buried in sheets not metre waves.

My absence makes my heart bloom fonder,
growing in size like envy at Christmas,
increasing in volume like the pounding in your
chest
whenever we meet again.
A wise ribcage steeling itself for a broken heart,
you hold me and it's as if we were never apart.

I wonder if our distance feels the same
in your hands, in your eyes and ears
as it does in mine, forlorn and watching the time.

BETWEEN THE TREES

We crash like cliffs and waves,
our love, a squall in the ocean's belly
in the middle of July.

And so, in your absence,
my skin is calm - untouched tranquillity
begging for a storm,
for you and me and the soar,
the chance to deafen a gull's screech
with the breath in our lungs.

At Night

I've tried to be better at this,
to miss you less.
I've tried not to fill every page
with my melancholy aches
or descriptions of how sullenly my heart
saunters in my chest,
looking for any remnant of you.

Always

I listen but do not watch
as you prepare to leave,
the closing of a cupboard door
a cymbal clatter to my ears;
resisting every note of goodbye –
shoes over socks, sighs
and the scratching of a key in the door –
holding on to the 'I love you'
whispered into my collarbone.
Hands clasped tightly in my lap,
reimagining the shawl of hope
and daydream you drew tightly
about my shoulders;
fingers palms arms of fabric,
when you vowed to keep me,
always.

January

When I say 'always'
I mean I will hold you
for months and months
of January
and weather every
winter in your heart.
I will ask Gaia if
all timeless loves must end
and their lovers, part –
if to be one
we must be two,
loving ourselves
before we can begin.
I will disregard her
words, anyway,
choosing sacrifice
and interminable seasons
of loss and loneliness
to find any way
you and I
can begin
and end
a cold December
together.

BETWEEN THE TREES

Thousand-Year-Old Forest

They had been lost on the road of undulating cobble stone for what could have been hours or years. The road was lined with trees; watched by a forest they daren't go near. From the outside they saw only darkness. They did not entertain the possibility of canopy free light. Adventurous spirit was too costly. Adventures into the unknown cleaved hearts in two and stole the breath from your chest. A risk could herald defeat in battle. It could be bruised knees and swollen feet. The forest appeared too dangerous but their hope deteriorated as the road flatlined into the horizon ahead.

She stopped. Stepped once to the side and then twice and thrice before her feet were entirely free of stone. She stood between the trees; heart drumming in its cage to the beat of the wind. She stood and she waited.

He stopped too; feet planted in stone, letting the wind whistle between them as the sky darkened. She had been the calm before his storm and now she was removed, stood in the shelter of the trees. The heavens opened and she flung her arms open.

BETWEEN THE TREES

Rivulets of rain slid from brow to collarbone. Shirt sodden, shoes soaked and heart heavy, he ran. He ran to the thousand-year-old forest and the woman at its edge. The woman who had decided she didn't want to make the bed unless one side belonged to him. She didn't want to walk another step unless it was with him, in the shade of the trees they had long forgotten.

You see in a forest like this, people discover the tastes, smells and person they choose to call 'Home'. Perfection doesn't live here but Hope does. Each trunk is weather beaten and each leaf has fallen but that doesn't stop the sun from shining or the storm from giving.

From the outside, Love is treacherous and unforgiving. But, if you take the time to wander a little, trace every lightning scar and curl into the arms flung open to you; you will learn Love is patient, Love is sturdy and it will wait for you, like a forest waits for Spring, to blossom and bloom.

KRISTIANA REED

IV

"I remember the she
in my poems and dreams,
is still me."

Whirligig

Aged Nine

There is a video of me
aged nine
with bobbed red hair
one finger in the air
waiting for the magician
to spin a plate.
I am wearing red
on my head, cheeks and heart
sparkles too
twiddling the tassels
at my neck.
What I would give
to step through the film
encase her in my warmth
remind her to smile
not to worry so
anxiously trying to be just so.

There is a video of me
aged nine
with bobbed red hair
a girl timid and fair
with much to bear.
What I would give
to step through the film
and tell her not to care.

Learning to braid

Years of painstaking practice had taught her fingers to interweave three strands of hair, into one cohesive thread. Just like how she'd pencilled birthdays into her mind. Just like how she'd learnt the knowing smile she needed to give your mother, an unspoken indictment of your forgetfulness when it came to saving a date. Just like how she knew every name you felt she needed to know, ready to say with lips pulled over the teeth you said she needed to show.

It took time to marry the strands; her hair was thin like silk and would often slip through her fingers. Or her arms grew tired, suspended behind her ears, biting her bottom lip trying to create perfection without a mirror. Just like how she patiently etched each facial expression of yours into her mind, only to read you wrong and pay in silence. Just like how she attempted to juggle the future you envisioned whilst walking on the tightrope of her ambition. Just like how she had begun to measure years, months, days and then hours of her life; living without a reflection.

Then there were the fly-aways. Wisps of unpredictability, spontaneity and reckless abandon furiously disobeying her sleight of hand. Whimsical kinks refusing to be held in one place or tied down amongst the rest; no matter how tight she pulled on the strands, no matter how many pins she buried deep into her hair. Just like her desire to spin out of orbit and taste oxygen with the excitement of never being able to again. Just like her attraction to his aftershave, his smile or his eyes. Just like her dream to free-fall into Fear instead of tuck it in at night, along with Time and Money.

Years of practice dispersed at once. The band which held it all together, snapped. The red ribbon, the lifeblood, came undone. The cohesive thread she'd worn like a badge of honour fell loosely about her shoulders and jaw. Strands she had forgotten about fell in front of her eyes and tickled her collar; rising and falling with shallow breaths of insecurity and hope. She'd spent years growing her hair so it was long enough to braid. Yet now, as it tumbled down the length of her spine, it felt weightless. She, felt weightless.

BETWEEN THE TREES

Whirligig

I used to believe
in abracadabra magic;
white rabbits from hats,
ribbons from shirt sleeves,
coins from behind my ear,
children's party make believe;
dragons and princesses,
tall towers and treehouses,
and the way the wind blows whispers
when you are small and slight
with dreams dripping on your brow
and in the crooks of your knees.

I used to believe
in the magic of me;
the sparkles in my eyes,
glitter in my smile
and magenta hope
pounding in my chest;
my audacity to just be
instead of want and worry.
Somewhere along the way
I lost the child in me;
forgot her on the journey home
from your heart to mine.
She was a whirligig

of reckless abandon,
ratty red hair beating the wind
stood at the top of the castle
with the cheesy grin
of a dirty rascal.

I used to believe
my magic was a memory
but as I sit by the sea,
to lose landlocked melancholy,
I remember the she
in my poems and dreams,
is still me.

Damsel

You are not a damsel in distress
nor a princess to be saved
you are a warrior
and you woke up like this;
beautiful in your fury,
stunning in your victory.
And if the tide flows red
and friend or foe
tries to treat you as less;
you show them the scars
of lightning - the livid
lily flesh of survival
not even Zeus can contest,
show them the fires
in your eyes
and thunderstorms
in your mind,
show them courage
in a smile or a scowl
because you are not
a damsel in distress
nor a princess to be saved,
you are blood and bones,
ink and hope;
breathing in spite
of the world.

BETWEEN THE TREES

Hope

Hope is like the tide;
even when all the way out,
it is on its way back to you.

Perennial Blossoms

I want to reach inside myself
and find perennial blossoms,
butterflies, and next times
living and breathing
in the sunlight
cast by my eyes
when I name each butterfly;
hope
courage
belief,
and every flower;
love
time
forgiveness,
and every next time;
tomorrow
tomorrow
tomorrow.

Enough

I wished for a mountain
with a babbling brook
a rock to climb
and a moment of calm,
where love, cannot touch you
except the swelling of your heart
as sunlight breaks through cloud
into bird song melody.

I dreamt of a forest
vast and crowded
with buzzing, bees and everything
in between,
where love, cannot find you
running through leaves
deeper into the moss.

I woke in a house
with brick walls
and plastered ceilings
at dawn, rosy and golden
a home and sanctuary,
in which love, was free
to touch and find me;
the girl who didn't realise,
she was enough.

Sand Heart

The princess was fast asleep;
the silence kept watch,
the stars kissed her goodnight
and the moon cuddled close
looming gently in the window,
cold breath caressing her cheeks,
pink in slumber
pale fingers closed over blankets,
a soft stream of fabric
tousled down her calves
bundled around her feet,
soft like her heart,
impressionable, sand
which refuses to let go
of the indecisive ocean.

Sometimes her father would return
to stand at her bedside
in starlight and shadow,
the moon bowing her head,
the stars blowing kisses
to fall upon his cheeks
flecked with grey,
a memento of the years
spent gazing into the night
for answers, and home

because each one he built
was never his own.

He watched his daughter instead;
found meaning in how her chest rose
with each flutter of breath,
found purpose in the one curl
which refused to lie
with the others cupping her chin,
found hope in her lashes
a delicate frame for the fierce love
glistening in her eyes.
He found a reason to live
when even clouds away,
drifting in dreams
he could never touch,
the corners of her mouth
twitched and whispered joy,
she smiled the smallest smile,
she smiled for him,
to save him;
her heart like sand
refusing to let go
of her ocean.

Inky Heaven

The gentle rumble of the stopped car
melted into the cold metal,
encasing the little woman,
wrapped in cotton
as her chin lifted skyward
slowly, moonlight on glass
caressing the sweetness
of her underside skin,
her eyes swelling with stars
dotted above her brow
in a sea of midnight,
a cloudless oasis
of wishes and meteorite.

Time passed as the world shifted
still with her gaze lifted
to an inky heaven swirled
with flickering light and love stories
played out for millennia;
a galaxy of kisses.

She grew cold in her rapture
held by a pin prick of light
already dying and yet
in the watercolour pools of her eyes,
the night sky had never looked so alive.

The Allotment

Three days had passed, since she visited her allotment last. She felt guilty for neglecting her parsnips, turnips, carrots, kale and cabbages. She hoped she would have prize-winners this year. She hoped for better than the disaster eleven months prior. The autumn she had succumbed to the fall. The weather had been exceptionally unkind. She was browbeaten by the wind and rain; and the fog still invaded her dreams at times.

She was adamant this year would be different. She would feign from hiding at home and letting indifference reign. And yet here she was again. The moment the sun had disappeared and waved goodbye to every colour of the rainbow in the flowerbeds; she too had taken to bed.

The guilt this time was unparalleled. In fact, she wondered if she would ever step back through the door. Whatever the weather. It didn't matter that some days the sun was wont to shine. One day in five wasn't enough to fight the ceaseless rain in her brain. Monsoon manacles which always chose shelter over pain. Her nights weaved images of wilting stems and curling leaves; tragic operatic notes blaring in every channel of her mind. Her mornings built her worries as high and thick as the metal fences and gates which were meant to keep her produce safe. But in her anxious day dreams she heard the sniffling of foxes and scratching of bugs; she heard the inevitable death of everything she loves.

Three days had passed in the vacuum of self-made eternity. She wondered if they missed her; as greenery turned to brown, folding over into the soil she had picked especially for a prosperous year. She wondered if plants felt betrayal; if they scowled as they gave her oxygen to breathe deep and calm but she choked and gasped, drowning on her future.

It took a nightmare flood to rip the bedsheets from her limbs. A wave of regret had swelled in the distance and rumbled down the road, before swishing gallantly around the corner to face the allotment, baring menacing sea foam bubbled teeth. The wave rolled forth; ripping trees from root, flattening shrubs and drowning flourishing vegetables and sleeping flowers.

The fourth day following a sleepless night brought her to the allotment gate. Greenery remained; flower buds bent in the breeze but were not bruised; leaves stretched toward the sun and did not curl inwards nor downward. Her absence was not tragic at all. Her return was welcomed kindly as her fingertips stroked the shrubs and tall, reaching plants as she passed. She sunk to her knees before the vegetable patch. She began to pull, gently and nervously.

Each pull revealed a result of her labour and love. Her hands were never left with just stalks and stems but were filled with hope and heavy with life. The weather had been bad but it had not been brutal. Her dreams were savage but they had not ruined the cabbage. Three days had passed but here she was at last. A survivor and a giver. Another year of lessons tucked mindfully into her gardening belt.

BETWEEN THE TREES

Kindness

This place
and its silence,
half-moon night sky and
second home kindness
taught me to wish
goodbye and love hello,
tucked me in a night,
whispered wishbone
hope into my ears
soothed all my fears;
tucked them in too,
left lavender,
on their pillows
called me home
and showed me mine.
poured love
from the stars
into my heart.
said I always was
a celestial being,
so I better
start believing
cradled me
in elastic arms
let me go
and found me.

BETWEEN THE TREES

Home

Ten more minutes and I'll be home.
Granny's old house
with a karaoke machine
in the cupboard under the stairs.
I'll have a bath
and ponder using the pumice stone
like I always did.
My evening will be spent
drinking tea from a mug
with a watercolour rabbit
and foxgloves on the side,
and eating toast,
barely toasted,
smothered in margarine.

BETWEEN THE TREES

Spring

A stem sprouts upward
pushing past tarmac to mock
the concrete jungle.

BETWEEN THE TREES

The Meadow

You are standing in a meadow,
it is lush green,
the kind people talk about
from the other side.
Life swells in pockets;
a city of daisies,
a bumblebee filling its knees,
tall tulips swaying in the breeze,
a buried village in the undergrowth
ants, woodlice and centipedes.
Sunshine weighs heavy
on your back,
on your shoulders,
your eyes water
and you cannot understand
what has brought you here;
to the edge of life in colour,
swimming in jewelled flowers,
the taste of pollen on your lips,
petals embracing the sun
the smell of hope –
poisonous joy.

You could step forward,
barefoot, unguarded
risking your soul for a chance

BETWEEN THE TREES

to choose the flowers
you adorn your home with.

Behind you is a forest,
its shadowy fingers lingering
about your waist
stretching toward your throat,
to regain its firm hold
on your senses and pull
you into the shade.
Life thrives here too, but unseen;
amber eyes become accustomed
to the night sky,
families burrow in the roots of great oaks,
hedgehogs find homes in autumn debris,
birds call and mate in the trees,
in the dust of your footsteps.
When you began, it was a stroll,
an amble into the unknown.
It grew dark with heavy boughs
as heavy as your chest,
threatening to end all light,
snuff out the life
under your collarbone.

At times you walked through clearings
and on the trees, you saw
faces, every one

*a loved one
but never yours.*

You're here, still standing
in a meadow
wondering what brought you
to this quiet place.
In the blue sky
there is a reflection
beckoning you forward.
She is kind,
she dreams in oranges and purples,
she believes in love,
she has led you here
past faces embedded in bark
to see yours, for once,
in the blinding sun.

BETWEEN THE TREES

KRISTIANA REED

Beyond the Trees

I will start and finish with being honest.
Apart from the wheat fields
and meadows in my dreams,
I struggle to imagine what it is like
beyond the trees.

Still, I would like to try.
I will begin with the wind;
there will be a breeze,
strong enough to flutter
the hem of a skirt
but too gentle to bend
branches and tug
at my limbs.
At times it will taste of the sea
and then of peaches –
no, nectarines,
because I've never liked the texture
of peach skin on my teeth.
It will tickle my cheeks and chin.
It will blow cloudy arms
around me as the earth
holds me.

The earth will be soft
as it always is, beneath my feet.

BETWEEN THE TREES

But this time I will feel steady;
on a grassy pavement, not a
telephone wire tightrope.
I will sink happily
to dig my fingers into the mud,
tuck the flowers in
and sing them to life.
I will hear the snuffles
of wildlife and breathe
a sigh of relief
that I'm not the only one here,
eyes watching the world go by,
rather than just the sky
through gaps in the trees.

I will look towards the forest edge,
smile and remember
fondly what it felt like
to be between the trees.
I will be thankful
for all their ageing wisdom
taught me. Although,
I will be thankful
to the powers that be
that I'm here now;
beyond the trees
with the sound of love
in my ears,

tears welling in my throat
and the taste of freedom,
long deserved,
on the tip of my tongue.

BETWEEN THE TREES

Acknowledgements

I am incredibly thankful for the people I have met in the lead up to publishing *Between the Trees*; from the teachers who pushed me to excel and inspired me, to the students I see every day who continue to push and inspire me.

My family and friends for the love, encouragement, library visits, book vouchers, note books and stationery.

Sarah, for writing the foreword and for being my mother and everything I could have wished for.

Nicholas, Kindra and Candice for believing in this book from the very beginning.

Everyone I have loved and lost; you've inspired the words in this book.

James, for being my unexpected partner in all things. This would not have happened without you.

*

And you, dear reader, for making every word worth it. Thank you.

About the author

Kristiana Reed is a writer and an English Teacher living in the UK. She is the creator of My Screaming Twenties on WordPress, a platform for her poetry, prose and book reviews. Her work has been published in several poetry anthologies (Swear To Me, All The Lonely People, We Will Not Be Silenced), in the feminist issue of MAELSTROM Zine and the inaugural issue (flight) from Nightingale and Sparrow.

Kristiana also runs Free Verse Revolution on WordPress; a site which shares the work of writers from all around the globe.

When she isn't teaching, writing or scheduling the work of others, you will find her reading, day dreaming, soaking up any tiny ray of British sun and cooing incessantly at her cat.

Printed in Great Britain
by Amazon